Concept created by Roger Price & Leonard Stern

PSS!

PRICE STERN SLOAN

An Imprint of Penguin Group (USA) Inc.

PRICE STERN SLOAN
Published by the Penguin Group

Penguin Group (USA) Inc., 375 Hudson Street, New York, New York 10014, USA
Penguin Group (Canada), 90 Eglinton Avenue East, Suite 700, Toronto, Ontario M4P 2Y3, Canada
(a division of Pearson Penguin Canada Inc.)
Penguin Books Ltd, 80 Strand, London WC2R 0RL, England
Penguin Ireland, 25 St Stephen's Green, Dublin 2, Ireland (a division of Penguin Books Ltd)
Penguin Group (Australia), 707 Collins Street, Melbourne, Victoria 3008, Australia
(a division of Pearson Australia Group Pty Ltd)
Penguin Books India Pvt Ltd, 11 Community Centre, Panchsheel Park, New Delhi—110 017, India
Penguin Group (NZ), 67 Apollo Drive, Rosedale, Auckland 0632, New Zealand
(a division of Pearson New Zealand Ltd)
Penguin Books (South Africa), Rosebank Office Park, 181 Jan Smuts Avenue,
Parktown North 2193, South Africa
Penguin China, B7 Jiaming Center, 27 East Third Ring Road North,
Chaoyang District, Beijing 100020, China

Penguin Books Ltd., Registered Offices:
80 Strand, London WC2R 0RL, England

MAD LIBS®
INSTRUCTIONS

MAD LIBS® is a game for people who don't like games! It can be played by one, two, three, four, or forty.

• RIDICULOUSLY SIMPLE DIRECTIONS

In this tablet you will find stories containing blank spaces where words are left out. One player, the READER, selects one of these stories. The READER does not tell anyone what the story is about. Instead, he/she asks the other players, the WRITERS, to give him/her words. These words are used to fill in the blank spaces in the story.

• TO PLAY

The READER asks each WRITER in turn to call out a word—an adjective or a noun or whatever the space calls for—and uses them to fill in the blank spaces in the story. The result is a MAD LIBS® game.

When the READER then reads the completed MAD LIBS® game to the other players, they will discover that they have written a story that is fantastic, screamingly funny, shocking, silly, crazy, or just plain dumb— depending upon which words each WRITER called out.

• EXAMPLE (*Before* and *After*)

" _____ !" he said _____
      EXCLAMATION   ADVERB

as he jumped into his convertible _____ and
                                        NOUN

drove off with his _____ wife.
                    ADJECTIVE

" *Ouch* !" he said *stupidly*
      EXCLAMATION   ADVERB

as he jumped into his convertible *cat* and
                                        NOUN

drove off with his *brave* wife.
                    ADJECTIVE

In case you have forgotten what adjectives, adverbs, nouns, and verbs are, here is a quick review:

An ADJECTIVE describes something or somebody. *Lumpy, soft, ugly, messy,* and *short* are adjectives.

An ADVERB tells how something is done. It modifies a verb and usually ends in "ly." *Modestly, stupidly, greedily,* and *carefully* are adverbs.

A NOUN is the name of a person, place, or thing. *Sidewalk, umbrella, bridle, bathtub,* and *nose* are nouns.

A VERB is an action word. *Run, pitch, jump,* and *swim* are verbs. Put the verbs in past tense if the directions say PAST TENSE. *Ran, pitched, jumped,* and *swam* are verbs in the past tense.

When we ask for A PLACE, we mean any sort of place: a country or city (*Spain, Cleveland*) or a room (*bathroom, kitchen*).

An EXCLAMATION or SILLY WORD is any sort of funny sound, gasp, grunt, or outcry, like *Wow!, Ouch!, Whomp!, Ick!,* and *Gadzooks!*

When we ask for specific words, like a NUMBER, a COLOR, an ANIMAL, or a PART OF THE BODY, we mean a word that is one of those things, like *seven, blue, horse,* or *head.*

When we ask for a PLURAL, it means more than one. For example, *cat* pluralized is *cats.*

MAD LIBS® is fun to play with friends, but you can also play it by yourself! To begin with, DO NOT look at the story on the page below. Fill in the blanks on this page with the words called for. Then, using the words you have selected, fill in the blank spaces in the story.

Now you've created your own hilarious MAD LIBS® game!

WELCOME TO SKYLANDS

ADJECTIVE _____

PLURAL NOUN _____

ADJECTIVE _____

A PLACE _____

NOUN _____

ADJECTIVE _____

NOUN _____

ADJECTIVE _____

NOUN _____

TYPE OF LIQUID _____

VERB ENDING IN "ING" _____

PLURAL NOUN _____

VERB _____

ADJECTIVE _____

PLURAL NOUN _____

PART OF THE BODY (PLURAL) _____

PLURAL NOUN _____

COLOR _____

VERB _____

MAD LIBS®
WELCOME TO SKYLANDS

Have you ever visited the _____ world known as
                            ADJECTIVE

Skylands? It's a cluster of floating _____ within a vast sea
                                      PLURAL NOUN

of _____ clouds, and it exists in the very center of (the)
     ADJECTIVE

_____. Magic flows from every rock, tree, and flower-covered
    A PLACE

_____ there. Inhabitants of this _____ place
       NOUN   ADJECTIVE

are known as Skylanders, and their mission is to protect the

_____ of Light, the greatest landmark in Skylands. It was
    NOUN

built long ago by the _____ Ancients to keep Skylands
                          ADJECTIVE

safe from a mysterious evil _____ known as the
                                 NOUN

Darkness. Skylands is an adventurer's paradise, with lagoons full of

_____ to go _____ in, ruins and
   TYPE OF LIQUID   VERB ENDING IN "ING"

_____ to explore, and lava pits and underground caves to
 PLURAL NOUN

_____ in. You'll encounter many _____ creatures in
   VERB   ADJECTIVE

Skylands. There are winged _____, trolls with hair growing
                               PLURAL NOUN

out of their _____, and fluffy white _____
              PART OF THE BODY (PLURAL)   PLURAL NOUN

roaming around the _____ pastures. Once you set foot in
                        COLOR

Skylands, you'll never want to _____!
                                   VERB

MAD LIBS® is fun to play with friends, but you can also play it by yourself! To begin with, DO NOT look at the story on the page below. Fill in the blanks on this page with the words called for. Then, using the words you have selected, fill in the blank spaces in the story.

Now you've created your own hilarious MAD LIBS® game!

WHO ARE
THE SKYLANDERS?

PLURAL NOUN _____

ADJECTIVE _____

NOUN _____

PLURAL NOUN _____

ADJECTIVE _____

VERB ENDING IN "ING" _____

NOUN _____

ADJECTIVE _____

PLURAL NOUN _____

ADVERB _____

PERSON IN ROOM _____

VERB (PAST TENSE) _____

NOUN _____

PLURAL NOUN _____

TYPE OF LIQUID _____

NOUN _____

PART OF THE BODY (PLURAL) _____

MAD LIBS®
WHO ARE THE SKYLANDERS?

The Skylanders are legendary fighting _____ whose mission
                                        PLURAL NOUN

is to protect their _____ home from an evil force known as
                      ADJECTIVE

the _____ by guarding the Core of Light. Using their magical
     NOUN

_____, _____ weaponry, and _____
PLURAL NOUN   ADJECTIVE   VERB ENDING IN "ING"

abilities, the Skylanders have defended their beloved _____
                                                        NOUN

for generations, keeping peace and order. The Skylanders live for

_____ action and love to battle _____. They are also
ADJECTIVE   PLURAL NOUN

_____ loyal to their leader, Master _____, possibly
ADVERB   PERSON IN ROOM

the greatest Portal Master who ever _____. Each
                                     VERB (PAST TENSE)

Skylander is powerful in a single Element, such as Earth, Fire, Water,

or _____. Depending on the Element, each Skylander has
    NOUN

a unique skill, like swinging flaming _____, spraying
                                        PLURAL NOUN

_____, throwing rocky _____-balls, or—one of the
TYPE OF LIQUID   NOUN

greatest but rarest skills—blasting lightning bolts from their

_____.
PART OF THE BODY (PLURAL)

From SKYLANDERS UNIVERSE MAD LIBS® • Skylanders Universe™ & © Activision Publishing, Inc.
Published by Price Stern Sloan, an imprint of Penguin Group (USA) Inc., 345 Hudson Street, New York, NY 10014.

MAD LIBS® is fun to play with friends, but you can also play it by yourself! To begin with, DO NOT look at the story on the page below. Fill in the blanks on this page with the words called for. Then, using the words you have selected, fill in the blank spaces in the story.

Now you've created your own hilarious MAD LIBS® game!

WHEN DARKNESS CAME

ADJECTIVE _____

NOUN _____

NOUN _____

TYPE OF LIQUID _____

PLURAL NOUN _____

PLURAL NOUN _____

PART OF THE BODY _____

VERB (PAST TENSE) _____

CELEBRITY _____

SAME CELEBRITY _____

ADJECTIVE _____

NOUN _____

PART OF THE BODY (PLURAL) _____

PLURAL NOUN _____

NOUN _____

A PLACE _____

PLURAL NOUN _____

ADJECTIVE _____

MAD LIBS®

WHEN DARKNESS CAME

One _____ day in Skylands, Spyro the purple _____
    ADJECTIVE   NOUN

and Gill Grunt, a/an _____-shooting fish creature, were
               NOUN

discussing how to spend the day. Should they go swimming in the hot

_____ pits or go exploring in the underground
   TYPE OF LIQUID

_____? Before they could decide, a swirl of dark, threatening
  PLURAL NOUN

_____ filled the sky, and suddenly there appeared a gigantic
  PLURAL NOUN

hooded _____ with glowing eyes that _____
    PART OF THE BODY   VERB (PAST TENSE)

in the most sinister way. It was the diabolical _____!
                          CELEBRITY

Although the Skylanders quickly banded together, they were no match

for _____'s _____ weapon, the Hydra, an enormous
  SAME CELEBRITY   ADJECTIVE

_____ with four _____ and viciously sharp
  NOUN   PART OF THE BODY (PLURAL)

_____! The Hydra destroyed the Core of Light, and a
  PLURAL NOUN

massive _____ exploded, causing the Skylanders to be
      NOUN

ejected toward (the) _____, where they reappeared as tiny
          A PLACE

_____. Will Skylands ever be _____ again?
  PLURAL NOUN   ADJECTIVE

MAD LIBS® is fun to play with friends, but you can also play it by yourself! To begin with, DO NOT look at the story on the page below. Fill in the blanks on this page with the words called for. Then, using the words you have selected, fill in the blank spaces in the story.

Now you've created your own hilarious MAD LIBS® game!

THE ELEMENTS-PART 1

ADJECTIVE _____

PLURAL NOUN _____

VERB _____

VERB _____

ADJECTIVE _____

ADJECTIVE _____

PLURAL NOUN _____

NOUN _____

CELEBRITY _____

ADJECTIVE _____

VERB _____

NOUN _____

TYPE OF LIQUID _____

PLURAL NOUN _____

PLURAL NOUN _____

PART OF THE BODY _____

MAD LIBS®
THE ELEMENTS-PART 1

Every Skylander has a/an _____ power connected with one of
                         ADJECTIVE
eight Elemental _____. These powers affect what they can do
                PLURAL NOUN
in battle—like _____ higher, _____ faster, or conjure
                  VERB   VERB
up super-_____ weapons. Some of the Elements include:
           ADJECTIVE

• **Magic**—Skylanders skilled in this Element use _____
                                                      ADJECTIVE

   sorcery or magical _____. The symbol of the Magic Element
                       PLURAL NOUN

   is stars and a/an _____. _____ the purple dragon is
                         NOUN   CELEBRITY

   the most famous of the Magic Skylanders.

• **Tech**—Technology is these Skylanders' _____ weapon. They
                                              ADJECTIVE

   can activate hidden mechanisms—like extending a bridge they can

   _____ on. The golden _____-slinger Trigger Happy
       VERB   NOUN

   is a Tech Skylander.

• **Fire**—Skylanders of this Element manipulate fire and molten

   _____ to burn down _____ and scorch enemy
   TYPE OF LIQUID   PLURAL NOUN

   _____. Eruptor is a Fire-based Skylander—and a total hot-
   PLURAL NOUN

   _____!
   PART OF THE BODY

MAD LIBS® is fun to play with friends, but you can also play it by yourself! To begin with, DO NOT look at the story on the page below. Fill in the blanks on this page with the words called for. Then, using the words you have selected, fill in the blank spaces in the story.

Now you've created your own hilarious MAD LIBS® game!

THE ELEMENTS-PART 2

ADJECTIVE _____

VERB _____

ADJECTIVE _____

ADJECTIVE _____

PLURAL NOUN _____

NOUN _____

PLURAL NOUN _____

ADJECTIVE _____

VERB ENDING IN "ING" _____

NOUN _____

VERB ENDING IN "ING" _____

PLURAL NOUN _____

ADJECTIVE _____

VERB _____

PLURAL NOUN _____

PLURAL NOUN _____

PART OF THE BODY (PLURAL) _____

The other _____ Elements are:
ADJECTIVE

* **Water**—Skylanders who wield this weapon can _____ in
  VERB

  any type of liquid. Gill Grunt is a/an _____ Water warrior.
  ADJECTIVE

* **Undead**—These Skylanders are often _____ skeletons or
  ADJECTIVE

  ghouls who use nonliving _____ in battle. The lightning-
  PLURAL NOUN

  breathing _____ Cynder is one.
  NOUN

* **Air**—These Skylanders use windy _____ and _____
  PLURAL NOUN   ADJECTIVE

  storms to fight. Jet-Vac is a daring _____ ace who can
  VERB ENDING IN "ING"

  fly with his _____.
  NOUN

* **Life**—Skylanders of this Element use living, _____
  VERB ENDING IN "ING"

  things, like plants or _____, to help them. The
  PLURAL NOUN

  _____ ninja Stealth Elf, known for her ability to
  ADJECTIVE

  _____ without making a sound, is one.
  VERB

* **Earth**—These Skylanders use rocks, soil, and _____ against
  PLURAL NOUN

  enemy _____. Prism Break is an Earth Skylander whose
  PLURAL NOUN

  rocky _____ wield powerful energy.
  PART OF THE BODY (PLURAL)

From SKYLANDERS UNIVERSE MAD LIBS® • Skylanders Universe™ & © Activision Publishing, Inc.
Published by Price Stern Sloan, an imprint of Penguin Group (USA) Inc., 345 Hudson Street, New York, NY 10014.

MAD LIBS® is fun to play with friends, but you can also play it by yourself! To begin with, DO NOT look at the story on the page below. Fill in the blanks on this page with the words called for. Then, using the words you have selected, fill in the blank spaces in the story.

Now you've created your own hilarious MAD LIBS® game!

WANTED: A FEW GOOD PORTAL MASTERS

ADJECTIVE _____

PLURAL NOUN _____

ADJECTIVE _____

CELEBRITY _____

PART OF THE BODY _____

TYPE OF LIQUID _____

PLURAL NOUN _____

NOUN _____

ADJECTIVE _____

ADJECTIVE _____

PLURAL NOUN _____

PLURAL NOUN _____

ADJECTIVE _____

A PLACE _____

NOUN _____

PART OF THE BODY (PLURAL) _____

VERB _____

MAD LIBS®
WANTED: A FEW GOOD PORTAL MASTERS

Do you possess the _____ ability to identify Skylanders with
 ADJECTIVE

powerful _____? Are you wise and all-_____? Do
 PLURAL NOUN   ADJECTIVE

you bear an uncanny resemblance to _____ when you grow a
 CELEBRITY

beard and strap a Viking helmet onto your _____? If so,
 PART OF THE BODY

then *you* just might have what it takes to be a Portal Master! While you

don't need royal _____ in your veins to qualify to be one, you
 TYPE OF LIQUID

do need a bank account with no less than one million

_____. The key to this job lies in having the power to
 PLURAL NOUN

control a Portal _____ and create a/an _____ bond
 NOUN   ADJECTIVE

with the Skylanders. As a Portal Master, you will guide the Skylanders

in their quest to explore _____ lands, battle menacing
 ADJECTIVE

_____, collect valuable _____, and solve
 PLURAL NOUN   PLURAL NOUN

_____ puzzles—all in the name of saving (the) _____!
 ADJECTIVE   A PLACE

Portal Masters are referred to as the "Great _____." The fate
 NOUN

of Skylands lies in your _____! If the job of a Portal
 PART OF THE BODY (PLURAL)

Master sounds right for you, _____ today for an application!
 VERB

MAD LIBS® is fun to play with friends, but you can also play it by yourself! To begin with, DO NOT look at the story on the page below. Fill in the blanks on this page with the words called for. Then, using the words you have selected, fill in the blank spaces in the story.

Now you've created your own hilarious MAD LIBS® game!

ATTACKING THE DARKNESS

PERSON IN ROOM _____

A PLACE _____

ADJECTIVE _____

PLURAL NOUN _____

NOUN _____

VERB ENDING IN "ING" _____

PLURAL NOUN _____

ADJECTIVE _____

ADJECTIVE _____

PLURAL NOUN _____

ANIMAL (PLURAL) _____

CELEBRITY (FEMALE) _____

ADJECTIVE _____

ADJECTIVE _____

PART OF THE BODY _____

VERB _____

ADJECTIVE _____

MAD LIBS®
ATTACKING THE DARKNESS

To defeat the despicable, bald-headed _____ and push the
PERSON IN ROOM

Darkness out of (the) _____ forever, you must guide your
A PLACE

Skylander to find these _____ items:
ADJECTIVE

- **Tiny colored** _____—These appear once an enemy
PLURAL NOUN

  _____ is beaten, and increase your Skylander's chance of
NOUN

  _____ in battle again.
VERB ENDING IN "ING"

- **Soul Gems**—These glowing, purple _____ can be used
PLURAL NOUN

  to unlock _____ upgraded powers for your Skylander.
ADJECTIVE

- _____ **Sapphires**—These floating blue _____
ADJECTIVE   PLURAL NOUN

  with wings look like weird, shiny _____ and can be used in
ANIMAL (PLURAL)

  the fairy _____'s shop located in the _____
CELEBRITY (FEMALE)   ADJECTIVE

  Ruins.

- **Hats**—These are much more than a/an _____ fashion
ADJECTIVE

  accessory. Pop a hat onto your Skylander's _____ to increase
PART OF THE BODY

  his speed, strength, and ability to _____. Hats can be large,
VERB

  small, funny, or _____.
ADJECTIVE

MAD LIBS® is fun to play with friends, but you can also play it by yourself! To begin with, DO NOT look at the story on the page below. Fill in the blanks on this page with the words called for. Then, using the words you have selected, fill in the blank spaces in the story.

Now you've created your own hilarious MAD LIBS® game!

BATTLE-MODE ARENAS

VERB ENDING IN "ING" _____

PART OF THE BODY _____

ADJECTIVE _____

VERB _____

PLURAL NOUN _____

PART OF THE BODY _____

NOUN _____

ADJECTIVE _____

PLURAL NOUN _____

VERB _____

TYPE OF LIQUID _____

NOUN _____

TYPE OF LIQUID _____

ADJECTIVE _____

PART OF THE BODY _____

Test your _____ skills by going head-to-_____
           VERB ENDING IN "ING"   PART OF THE BODY

with other Skylanders at these locations. As the saying goes, practice

makes _____!
        ADJECTIVE

• **Cyclops Square**—Test your Skylander's abilities to spar, but don't

   _____ in one place for too long. Otherwise, sharp
          VERB

   _____ will thrust up from under the floor and stab your
   PLURAL NOUN

   Skylander right in the _____—ouch!
                           PART OF THE BODY

• **Mushroom Grove**—This pasturelike _____ is quiet, grassy,
                                        NOUN

   and _____—but beware of the exploding _____!
          ADJECTIVE   PLURAL NOUN

• **Aqueduct**—Use the bounce pads to help your Skylander

   _____ to higher ground. Watch out for the Hazard
          VERB

   Activators—they will flood the Aqueduct with _____!
                                                  TYPE OF LIQUID

• **Troll Factory**—This colorful arena features conveyor belts and a

   metal _____ suspended over boiling _____. Avoid
            NOUN   TYPE OF LIQUID

   the _____ flame jets, though! After all, your Skylander
          ADJECTIVE

   can't battle with a burned _____!
                               PART OF THE BODY

From SKYLANDERS UNIVERSE MAD LIBS® • Skylanders Universe™ & © Activision Publishing, Inc.
Published by Price Stern Sloan, an imprint of Penguin Group (USA) Inc., 345 Hudson Street, New York, NY 10014.

MAD LIBS® is fun to play with friends, but you can also play it by yourself! To begin with, DO NOT look at the story on the page below. Fill in the blanks on this page with the words called for. Then, using the words you have selected, fill in the blank spaces in the story.

Now you've created your own hilarious MAD LIBS® game!

SKYLANDER SMACKDOWN

ADJECTIVE _____

NOUN _____

ADVERB _____

NOUN _____

NUMBER _____

PART OF THE BODY _____

EXCLAMATION _____

VERB _____

ADJECTIVE _____

NOUN _____

VERB _____

VERB _____

TYPE OF LIQUID _____

ADJECTIVE _____

NOUN _____

PART OF THE BODY _____

VERB _____

MAD●LIBS®
SKYLANDER SMACKDOWN

In a duel between fish warrior Gill Grunt and the silent-but-
_____ Stealth Elf, who will be the last _____ standing?
ADJECTIVE   NOUN

Portal Master 1: That was a/an _____ awesome maneuver
                                         ADVERB

by Gill Grunt! He twirled his _____-shaped harpoon and
                                   NOUN

came within _____ inches of jabbing Stealth Elf right in her
               NUMBER

_____! _____!
PART OF THE BODY   EXCLAMATION

Portal Master 2: Oh! But she used her ability to _____ into
                                                      VERB

thin air and left a/an _____ decoy in her place. She reappeared
                          ADJECTIVE

behind her opponent and slashed at him with her razor-sharp

_____! Ha-ha—you can run, but you can't _____!
NOUN   VERB

Portal Master 1: No—but he can fly! He managed to hit the

"_____" button on his _____ jetpack and fly out of
VERB   TYPE OF LIQUID

the way just in the nick of time. Incredible!

Portal Master 2: Not to be outdone, Stealth Elf executed a series of

_____ backflips across the _____ and _____-
ADJECTIVE   NOUN   PART OF THE BODY

slams Gill Grunt! You _____, girl!
                          VERB

From SKYLANDERS UNIVERSE MAD LIBS® • Skylanders Universe™ & © Activision Publishing, Inc.
Published by Price Stern Sloan, an imprint of Penguin Group (USA) Inc., 345 Hudson Street, New York, NY 10014.

MAD LIBS® is fun to play with friends, but you can also play it by yourself! To begin with, DO NOT look at the story on the page below. Fill in the blanks on this page with the words called for. Then, using the words you have selected, fill in the blank spaces in the story.

Now you've created your own hilarious MAD LIBS® game!

ODE TO BEING EVIL, BY KAOS

ADJECTIVE _____

VERB _____

ADJECTIVE _____

PLURAL NOUN _____

VERB ENDING IN "ING" _____

PART OF THE BODY _____

VERB _____

ADJECTIVE _____

NOUN _____

COLOR _____

PART OF THE BODY _____

VERB ENDING IN "ING" _____

PART OF THE BODY _____

ADJECTIVE _____

CELEBRITY _____

ODE TO BEING EVIL,
BY KAOS

First gather a/an _____ army to _____ and to fight;
ADJECTIVE / VERB

Include _____ minions—like Chompies that bite!
ADJECTIVE

Cackling _____ have deadly _____ powers,
PLURAL NOUN / VERB ENDING IN "ING"

While the cyclops's one _____ makes anything cower!
PART OF THE BODY

Train Trolls to _____ fiercely, teach spell punks to cast spells.
VERB

With _____ imps at your side, all will go well!
ADJECTIVE

Next apply a/an _____-shaped _____ tattoo
NOUN / COLOR

Right to your _____—it's what villains do!
PART OF THE BODY

Practice _____ evilly to make Skylanders cry;
VERB ENDING IN "ING"

Project a giant _____ up in the night sky!
PART OF THE BODY

Last but not least, find a/an _____ sidekick—
ADJECTIVE

I tried for _____, but Glumshanks did the trick.
CELEBRITY

From SKYLANDERS UNIVERSE MAD LIBS® • Skylanders Universe™ & © Activision Publishing, Inc.
Published by Price Stern Sloan, an imprint of Penguin Group (USA) Inc., 345 Hudson Street, New York, NY 10014.

MAD LIBS® is fun to play with friends, but you can also play it by yourself! To begin with, DO NOT look at the story on the page below. Fill in the blanks on this page with the words called for. Then, using the words you have selected, fill in the blank spaces in the story.

Now you've created your own hilarious MAD LIBS® game!

PORTAL TRAVEL TIPS

ADJECTIVE _____

PLURAL NOUN _____

NOUN _____

ADJECTIVE _____

VERB (PAST TENSE) _____

ADJECTIVE _____

PLURAL NOUN _____

VERB ENDING IN "ING" _____

PART OF THE BODY (PLURAL) _____

VERB _____

ANIMAL (PLURAL) _____

ADJECTIVE _____

TYPE OF LIQUID _____

MAD LIBS®
PORTAL TRAVEL TIPS

Portals are _____ doorways that connect two _____
        ADJECTIVE   PLURAL NOUN

in space and time. As a/an _____ Master, it's important to
                                    NOUN

teach your Skylanders the safe way to travel by Portal. It's not as

_____ as it looks! Here are step-by-step instructions:
   ADJECTIVE

1. Skylanders must have _____ for at least eight hours so
                          VERB (PAST TENSE)

   they are well rested. They should also be well fed on _____
                                                              ADJECTIVE

   battle-ready snacks, such as watermelon, pretzels, and cheese-

   flavored _____.
            PLURAL NOUN

2. Be sure the Skylanders are standing in a/an _____
                                                VERB ENDING IN "ING"

   position on the Portal.

3. Once teleporting begins, the Skylanders must clench their

   _____ together as tightly as possible and
   PART OF THE BODY (PLURAL)

   _____ steadily while counting _____.
        VERB   ANIMAL (PLURAL)

4. As Skylanders travel through a Portal, it's customary for them to yell

   out a/an _____ battle cry. In fact, there's an annual contest
              ADJECTIVE

   to see whose cry is the loudest and the best at making _____
                                                           TYPE OF LIQUID

   shoot out of people's noses in terror.

From SKYLANDERS UNIVERSE MAD LIBS® • Skylanders Universe™ & © Activision Publishing, Inc.
Published by Price Stern Sloan, an imprint of Penguin Group (USA) Inc., 345 Hudson Street, New York, NY 10014.

MAD LIBS® is fun to play with friends, but you can also play it by yourself! To begin with, DO NOT look at the story on the page below. Fill in the blanks on this page with the words called for. Then, using the words you have selected, fill in the blank spaces in the story.

Now you've created your own hilarious MAD LIBS® game!

ENEMIES 101

ADJECTIVE _____

NOUN _____

VERB _____

VERB _____

NOUN _____

ADJECTIVE _____

PLURAL NOUN _____

PLURAL NOUN _____

PART OF THE BODY (PLURAL) _____

PLURAL NOUN _____

ADJECTIVE _____

TYPE OF LIQUID _____

PLURAL NOUN _____

PLURAL NOUN _____

NOUN _____

ADJECTIVE _____

ARTICLE OF CLOTHING (PLURAL) _____

MAD☺LIBS®
ENEMIES 101

Skylanders must know their _____ enemies. It seems like
                     ADJECTIVE

each _____ is more dangerous than the last—so the best
       NOUN

strategy is to _____ first, ask questions later!
          VERB

- **Chompies** bark and _____ like dogs and will bite your
                    VERB

  _____ off—literally!
  NOUN

- **The Drow** are _____ elves who have embraced the dark
              ADJECTIVE

  _____. There are several different types, like Goliath Drows,
  PLURAL NOUN

  who attack Skylanders with spiked _____ attached to their
                            PLURAL NOUN

  _____.
  PART OF THE BODY (PLURAL)

- **Spell punks** are magical _____ who use their
                         PLURAL NOUN

  _____ powers to cause mischief. When defeated, they
  ADJECTIVE

  disappear in a *POOF!* of magical _____.
                           TYPE OF LIQUID

- **Imps** are feisty little _____ that do damage with weapons
                PLURAL NOUN

  such as burning _____ and mini-_____ launchers.
          PLURAL NOUN   NOUN

- **Trolls** are _____ bullies who like to hide bombs in one
           ADJECTIVE

  another's _____.
     ARTICLE OF CLOTHING (PLURAL)

MAD LIBS® is fun to play with friends, but you can also play it by yourself! To begin with, DO NOT look at the story on the page below. Fill in the blanks on this page with the words called for. Then, using the words you have selected, fill in the blank spaces in the story.

Now you've created your own hilarious MAD LIBS® game!

THE FANTASTIC FLYING FLYNN

A PLACE _____

CELEBRITY (MALE) _____

NOUN _____

ADJECTIVE _____

PART OF THE BODY (PLURAL) _____

NOUN _____

CELEBRITY (FEMALE) _____

PLURAL NOUN _____

ADJECTIVE _____

NOUN _____

VERB _____

NOUN _____

VERB ENDING IN "ING" _____

NOUN _____

MAD LIBS®
THE FANTASTIC FLYING FLYNN

The name's Flynn—and I am the greatest balloonist in all of (the)

_____! You've probably heard of me; I'm generally regarded

A PLACE

as Skylands' own version of _____. With the stylish pilot's

CELEBRITY (MALE)

_____ that I like to parade around in, plus the ultra-

NOUN

_____ goggles that I wear on my _____, I

ADJECTIVE   PART OF THE BODY (PLURAL)

am one impressive _____, if I do say so myself. I don't

NOUN

want to brag, but I helped save that cute Mabu _____

CELEBRITY (FEMALE)

from the enemy _____ holding her captive in Perilous

PLURAL NOUN

Pastures. I'm sure she was in awe of me—and who could blame her?

I may not be a Skylander, but I'm every bit as _____ of a hero

ADJECTIVE

as they are. That Kaos is a devilish _____, and whatever I

NOUN

can do to help make sure he will never _____ again, I'll

VERB

do it! I'll use my hot air _____ to take the Skylanders

NOUN

wherever they need to go to fight Kaos. When it comes to successfully

_____ across the skies of Skylands, I'm your

VERB ENDING IN "ING"

_____.

NOUN

MAD LIBS® is fun to play with friends, but you can also play it by yourself! To begin with, DO NOT look at the story on the page below. Fill in the blanks on this page with the words called for. Then, using the words you have selected, fill in the blank spaces in the story.

Now you've created your own hilarious MAD LIBS® game!

HOW TO RESTORE THE CORE OF LIGHT, BY HUGO

ADJECTIVE _____

CELEBRITY _____

A PLACE _____

VERB ENDING IN "ING" _____

PART OF THE BODY _____

ADJECTIVE _____

NOUN _____

ADVERB _____

NOUN _____

PLURAL NOUN _____

ADJECTIVE _____

TYPE OF LIQUID _____

PLURAL NOUN _____

ADJECTIVE _____

TYPE OF LIQUID _____

TYPE OF LIQUID _____

Hello there—I am Hugo, the _____ assistant to the greatest
ADJECTIVE

Portal Master of all time, _____. As the resident historian of
CELEBRITY

(the) _____, I can often be found _____
A PLACE VERB ENDING IN "ING"

aimlessly with my _____ buried in a book. I am not a
PART OF THE BODY

fighter—why, I wouldn't even know the difference between a/an

_____ weapon and a regular _____! But I am
ADJECTIVE NOUN

_____ knowledgeable about other things—like how to repair
ADVERB

the _____ of Light. Did you know that the Core was
NOUN

constructed using different _____ found all around Skylands
PLURAL NOUN

and is powered by all the _____ Elements? I'll just use my Far
ADJECTIVE

Viewer to help the Skylanders find the Eternal Sources, including

Air, Earth, _____, Fire, Magic, and _____. They also
TYPE OF LIQUID PLURAL NOUN

need to find other parts, like the _____ Gear that operates the
ADJECTIVE

Core's clockwork, the Green Primordial _____ to grease it,
TYPE OF LIQUID

and Quicksilver, an ancient _____ that is the essence of all
TYPE OF LIQUID

magical beings. Once all the Elements are found, we'll be good to go—

the Core can be restored!

MAD LIBS® is fun to play with friends, but you can also play it by yourself! To begin with, DO NOT look at the story on the page below. Fill in the blanks on this page with the words called for. Then, using the words you have selected, fill in the blank spaces in the story.

Now you've created your own hilarious MAD LIBS® game!

NEW HEROIC CHALLENGES

NOUN _____

VERB ENDING IN "ING" _____

ADJECTIVE _____

PERSON IN ROOM _____

ADJECTIVE _____

CELEBRITY _____

NOUN _____

ANIMAL (PLURAL) _____

PART OF THE BODY _____

NOUN _____

CELEBRITY _____

ADJECTIVE _____

TYPE OF FOOD (PLURAL) _____

PLURAL NOUN _____

PART OF THE BODY _____

PLURAL NOUN _____

ADJECTIVE _____

PLURAL NOUN _____

TYPE OF LIQUID _____

MAD LIBS®
NEW HEROIC CHALLENGES

I'm Cali, and as the _____ in charge of Heroic Challenges for
                          NOUN

all the Skylanders, I'm here to tell you these _____
                                               VERB ENDING IN "ING"

missions are as tough and as _____ as I am! Here are some
                              ADJECTIVE

new ones I'm planning for a rookie Skylander named _____:
                                                   PERSON IN ROOM

• Destroy all the _____ statues that look like _____.
                   ADJECTIVE   CELEBRITY

• Clear the forested _____ of all the giant _____.
                     NOUN   ANIMAL (PLURAL)

• Jump up and down on one _____ collecting
                          PART OF THE BODY

  _____-shaped charms.
   NOUN

• Rescue _____ from the _____ Trolls by attacking
          CELEBRITY   ADJECTIVE

  them with exploding _____.
                      TYPE OF FOOD (PLURAL)

• Break as many brick _____ as you can using only your
                      PLURAL NOUN

  _____.
  PART OF THE BODY

• Retrieve the ancient book of _____ from the _____
                               PLURAL NOUN   ADJECTIVE

  spell punks.

• Squeeze juicy _____ until you find the one that oozes
                PLURAL NOUN

  _____, and then drink it down—*yum*!
  TYPE OF LIQUID

From SKYLANDERS UNIVERSE MAD LIBS® • Skylanders Universe™ & © Activision Publishing, Inc.
Published by Price Stern Sloan, an imprint of Penguin Group (USA) Inc., 345 Hudson Street, New York, NY 10014.

MAD LIBS® is fun to play with friends, but you can also play it by yourself! To begin with, DO NOT look at the story on the page below. Fill in the blanks on this page with the words called for. Then, using the words you have selected, fill in the blank spaces in the story.

Now you've created your own hilarious MAD LIBS® game!

A GIANT STEP FORWARD

PLURAL NOUN _____

ADJECTIVE _____

PLURAL NOUN _____

ADJECTIVE _____

A PLACE _____

CELEBRITY (MALE) _____

ADJECTIVE _____

PLURAL NOUN _____

ADJECTIVE _____

VERB _____

PLURAL NOUN _____

PART OF THE BODY (PLURAL) _____

VERB (PAST TENSE) _____

PART OF THE BODY _____

VERB _____

A GIANT STEP FORWARD

According to the history of Skylands, giant _____ were the
PLURAL NOUN

original protectors of Skylands. These giants conquered the Arkeyans,

a/an _____ ancient race of evil robotic _____. But
ADJECTIVE PLURAL NOUN

their victory came with a price, as the _____ giants were
ADJECTIVE

banished to (the) _____, where they remained for ten thousand
A PLACE

years. When the power-hungry Portal Master _____
CELEBRITY (MALE)

returned for the second time to try to defeat the Skylanders, he

reawakened the Arkeyans to help him in his _____ quest to
ADJECTIVE

rule over Skylands. Faced with these threats, the Skylanders summoned

the giant _____ to join forces. The giants proved to be
PLURAL NOUN

_____ allies, with their abilities to throw, _____,
ADJECTIVE VERB

and destroy huge objects such as trees, boulders, and _____
PLURAL NOUN

using only their bare _____! Their enormous size
PART OF THE BODY (PLURAL)

caused the ground to shake whenever they _____,
VERB (PAST TENSE)

leaving giant _____-prints wherever they went. With the
PART OF THE BODY

giants by their side, the Skylanders were able to _____ their
VERB

way to victory and save Skylands again!

From SKYLANDERS UNIVERSE MAD LIBS® • Skylanders Universe™ & © Activision Publishing, Inc.
Published by Price Stern Sloan, an imprint of Penguin Group (USA) Inc., 345 Hudson Street, New York, NY 10014.

MAD LIBS® is fun to play with friends, but you can also play it by yourself! To begin with, DO NOT look at the story on the page below. Fill in the blanks on this page with the words called for. Then, using the words you have selected, fill in the blank spaces in the story.

Now you've created your own hilarious MAD LIBS® game!

WEAPONS CHECK

ADJECTIVE _____

PART OF THE BODY (PLURAL) _____

PLURAL NOUN _____

ADJECTIVE _____

PART OF THE BODY (PLURAL) _____

ADJECTIVE _____

PART OF THE BODY _____

PLURAL NOUN _____

ADJECTIVE _____

PLURAL NOUN _____

ANIMAL _____

VERB ENDING IN "ING" _____

ADJECTIVE _____

PLURAL NOUN _____

NOUN _____

ADJECTIVE _____

MAD LIBS®
WEAPONS CHECK

Some of the Skylanders' weapons are as unusual as they are

_____. For example, sometimes their weapons are actually
ADJECTIVE

part of their bodies—like in the case of Stump Smash, whose

_____ are actually large tree stumps that can
PART OF THE BODY (PLURAL)

pound the _____ out of Trolls. Slam Bam is armed and
PLURAL NOUN

_____, wielding four frozen _____ that
ADJECTIVE   PART OF THE BODY (PLURAL)

unleash some icy damage. Wrecking Ball has a/an _____,
ADJECTIVE

lethal tongue that unrolls from his _____ to give his
PART OF THE BODY

opposing _____ a licking—literally! Other Skylanders
PLURAL NOUN

have more traditional weapons. For example, Flameslinger is a/an

_____ blindfolded archer who shoots flaming
ADJECTIVE

_____ at enemies. Warnado is a hard-shelled _____
PLURAL NOUN   ANIMAL

known for _____ with the dizzying, deadly speed of
VERB ENDING IN "ING"

a/an _____ tornado. Ghost Roaster mows down rows of
ADJECTIVE

_____ with a spiked _____ on a chain. When it
PLURAL NOUN   NOUN

comes to a weapon-wielding Skylander, beware—or be _____!
ADJECTIVE

From SKYLANDERS UNIVERSE MAD LIBS® • Skylanders Universe™ & © Activision Publishing, Inc.
Published by Price Stern Sloan, an imprint of Penguin Group (USA) Inc., 345 Hudson Street, New York, NY 10014.

MAD LIBS® is fun to play with friends, but you can also play it by yourself! To begin with, DO NOT look at the story on the page below. Fill in the blanks on this page with the words called for. Then, using the words you have selected, fill in the blank spaces in the story.

Now you've created your own hilarious MAD LIBS® game!

THE GIANTS–PART 1

PERSON IN ROOM _____

ADJECTIVE _____

NOUN _____

VERB ENDING IN "ING" _____

ADJECTIVE _____

TYPE OF LIQUID _____

NOUN _____

NOUN _____

ADJECTIVE _____

PART OF THE BODY _____

PART OF THE BODY _____

ADJECTIVE _____

PLURAL NOUN _____

VERB _____

PLURAL NOUN _____

NOUN _____

PERSON IN ROOM _____

TYPE OF LIQUID _____

NOUN _____

MAD LIBS®
THE GIANTS-PART 1

When the Skylanders needed help taking down the evil

_____, they turned to some _____ supersize allies:
　　PERSON IN ROOM　　　　　　　　　　　ADJECTIVE

- **Tree Rex** is a giant mutant _____ who was once a regular
　　　　　　　　　　　　　　　　　NOUN

  tree _____ peacefully in a/an _____ forest.
　　　VERB ENDING IN "ING"　　　　　　　　ADJECTIVE

  An Arkeyan factory oozed poisonous _____ that altered
　　　　　　　　　　　　　　　　　TYPE OF LIQUID

  him. He uses his bark-encrusted _____ to smash things.
　　　　　　　　　　　　　　　　NOUN

- **Bouncer** is a security _____ and former _____
　　　　　　　　　　　　NOUN　　　　　　　　　　　ADJECTIVE

  Roboto Ball player. His weapons include _____-guns and
　　　　　　　　　　　　　　　　　　PART OF THE BODY

  _____-mounted rockets.
　PART OF THE BODY

- **Swarm** is a bee and comes from a race of _____ insect
　　　　　　　　　　　　　　　　　　　　ADJECTIVE

  warriors. He uses sharp _____ to attack enemies and can
　　　　　　　　　　　　　PLURAL NOUN

  _____ in the air and fight from above.
　　VERB

- **Crusher** is formed from rocky _____. He attacks with a
　　　　　　　　　　　　　　　PLURAL NOUN

  rock-crushing _____ that he named _____ .
　　　　　　　　　NOUN　　　　　　　　　　　PERSON IN ROOM

  He can shoot lasers of icy _____ from his goggles and
　　　　　　　　　　　　　TYPE OF LIQUID

  can self-destruct into small chunks of _____.
　　　　　　　　　　　　　　　　　　NOUN

From SKYLANDERS UNIVERSE MAD LIBS® • Skylanders Universe™ & © Activision Publishing, Inc.
Published by Price Stern Sloan, an imprint of Penguin Group (USA) Inc., 345 Hudson Street, New York, NY 10014.

MAD LIBS® is fun to play with friends, but you can also play it by yourself! To begin with, DO NOT look at the story on the page below. Fill in the blanks on this page with the words called for. Then, using the words you have selected, fill in the blank spaces in the story.

Now you've created your own hilarious MAD LIBS® game!

THE GIANTS-PART 2

ADJECTIVE _____

NOUN _____

ADJECTIVE _____

ADJECTIVE _____

PART OF THE BODY _____

ADJECTIVE _____

NOUN _____

VERB ENDING IN "ING" _____

VERB _____

ADJECTIVE _____

NOUN _____

PART OF THE BODY _____

NOUN _____

NOUN _____

TYPE OF LIQUID _____

TYPE OF FOOD _____

Here are some more _____ giants:
ADJECTIVE

• **Thumpback** is a humpbacked _____ who once served
NOUN

on a/an _____ pirate ship. He attacks with a/an
ADJECTIVE

_____ anchor and a deadly _____-flop.
ADJECTIVE   PART OF THE BODY

• **Ninjini** was a well-known magical ninja—until a/an _____
ADJECTIVE

sorceress trapped her inside an enchanted glass _____. While
NOUN

imprisoned, Ninjini mastered the art of sword _____.
VERB ENDING IN "ING"

Besides hacking with her swords, she can also _____ inside
VERB

her bottle and blast out in a/an _____ magical explosion.
ADJECTIVE

• **Eye-Brawl** is a headless giant with one huge _____ where
NOUN

his _____ should be! His attacks include punches and the
PART OF THE BODY

ability to detach his _____ from his body and fly around
NOUN

shooting _____ lasers.
NOUN

• **Hot Head** is a fire creature filled with magical, flammable

_____. His attacks include shooting flames and launching
TYPE OF LIQUID

blobs of burning _____.
TYPE OF FOOD

MAD LIBS® is fun to play with friends, but you can also play it by yourself! To begin with, DO NOT look at the story on the page below. Fill in the blanks on this page with the words called for. Then, using the words you have selected, fill in the blank spaces in the story.

Now you've created your own hilarious MAD LIBS® game!

FACE-OFF WITH KAOS

ADJECTIVE _____

NOUN _____

CELEBRITY _____

PLURAL NOUN _____

ADJECTIVE _____

PLURAL NOUN _____

ADJECTIVE _____

ADJECTIVE _____

PLURAL NOUN _____

NOUN _____

PART OF THE BODY (PLURAL) _____

VERB _____

EXCLAMATION _____

NOUN _____

PERSON IN ROOM _____

NOUN _____

A PLACE _____

PLURAL NOUN _____

It's all come down to this—a/an _____, epic battle between

ADJECTIVE

the heroic Skylanders and their arch-_____, Kaos, at his lair.

NOUN

Led by _____ the dragon, the Skylanders fight Kaos in his

CELEBRITY

death machine while tornado-shaped _____ whirl nearby.

PLURAL NOUN

Waves of _____ minions attack our heroes with magic green

ADJECTIVE

_____, laser beams, and _____ fireballs. Wait—

PLURAL NOUN   ADJECTIVE

what's this?! Kaos has just summoned the most _____ and

ADJECTIVE

powerful of all his _____, the deadly four-headed

PLURAL NOUN

_____! If the Skylanders manage to get out of this, it will be

NOUN

by the skin of their _____! The Skylanders

PART OF THE BODY (PLURAL)

_____ with all their strength and cunning—and

VERB

_____!—what do you know?! They defeat the Hydra—

EXCLAMATION

and that dastardly little _____, _____! They

NOUN   PERSON IN ROOM

enclose him in a golden _____, and Master Eon sends

NOUN

him to (the) _____. Well, as the saying goes, good riddance

A PLACE

to bad _____!

PLURAL NOUN

MAD LIBS® is fun to play with friends, but you can also play it by yourself! To begin with, DO NOT look at the story on the page below. Fill in the blanks on this page with the words called for. Then, using the words you have selected, fill in the blank spaces in the story.

Now you've created your own hilarious MAD LIBS® game!

ONE-ON-ONE WITH SPYRO

PLURAL NOUN _____

ADJECTIVE _____

TYPE OF LIQUID _____

NOUN _____

ADJECTIVE _____

VERB _____

NOUN _____

PLURAL NOUN _____

ADJECTIVE _____

NOUN _____

PART OF THE BODY _____

ADJECTIVE _____

A PLACE _____

NOUN _____

NOUN _____

MAD LIBS®

ONE-ON-ONE WITH SPYRO

After the dust had settled and the _____ had cleared, a/an
<u>PLURAL NOUN</u>

_____ Spyro and Master Eon discussed Kaos's downfall over
<u>ADJECTIVE</u>

a glass of frothy _____.
<u>TYPE OF LIQUID</u>

Master Eon: Spyro, my _____, this was a close call for
<u>NOUN</u>

Skylands! Did you think things looked so _____ that the
<u>ADJECTIVE</u>

Skylanders would _____ in the end?
<u>VERB</u>

Spyro: Totally! The Hydra's _____ once got so close to me
<u>NOUN</u>

that I could feel its breath—which smelled like rotten _____.
<u>PLURAL NOUN</u>

Master Eon: What did you think was the _____ turning
<u>ADJECTIVE</u>

point for you and your fellow Skylanders?

Spyro: When Trigger Happy shot a golden _____ into the
<u>NOUN</u>

Hydra's _____.
<u>PART OF THE BODY</u>

Master Eon: Any final _____ words for your archenemy?
<u>ADJECTIVE</u>

Spyro: I hope you rot in (the) _____, you lousy _____!
<u>A PLACE</u> <u>NOUN</u>

Master Eon: What will you do to celebrate?

Spyro: We're going to _____ Land!
<u>NOUN</u>

From SKYLANDERS UNIVERSE MAD LIBS® • Skylanders Universe™ & © Activision Publishing, Inc.
Published by Price Stern Sloan, an imprint of Penguin Group (USA) Inc., 345 Hudson Street, New York, NY 10014.

This book is published by

PSS!

PRICE STERN SLOAN

whose other splendid titles include
such literary classics as

Ad Lib Mad Libs®
Best of Mad Libs®
Camp Daze Mad Libs®
Christmas Carol Mad Libs®
Christmas Fun Mad Libs®
Cool Mad Libs®
Dance Mania Mad Libs®
Dear Valentine Letters Mad Libs®
Dinosaur Mad Libs®
Diva Girl Mad Libs®
Dude, Where's My Mad Libs®
Easter Eggstravaganza Mad Libs®
Family Tree Mad Libs®
Fun in the Sun Mad Libs®
Girls Just Wanna Have Mad Libs®
Goofy Mad Libs®
Grab Bag Mad Libs®
Graduation Mad Libs®
Grand Slam Mad Libs®
Hanukkah Mad Libs®
Happily Ever Mad Libs®
Happy Birthday Mad Libs®
Haunted Mad Libs®
Holly, Jolly Mad Libs®
Hot Off the Presses Mad Libs®
Kid Libs Mad Libs®
Letters from Camp Mad Libs®
Letters to Mom & Dad Mad Libs®
Mad About Animals Mad Libs®

Mad Libs® for President
Mad Libs® from Outer Space
Mad Libs® in Love
Mad Libs® on the Road
Mad Mad Mad Mad Mad Libs®
Monster Mad Libs®
More Best of Mad Libs®
Night of the Living Mad Libs®
Ninjas Mad Libs®
Off-the-Wall Mad Libs®
The Original #1 Mad Libs®
P. S. I Love Mad Libs®
Peace, Love, and Mad Libs®
Pirates Mad Libs®
Prime-Time Mad Libs®
Rock 'n' Roll Mad Libs®
Slam Dunk Mad Libs®
Sleepover Party Mad Libs®
Son of Mad Libs®
Sooper Dooper Mad Libs®
Spooky Mad Libs®
Straight "A" Mad Libs®
Totally Pink Mad Libs®
Undead Mad Libs®
Upside Down Mad Libs®
Vacation Fun Mad Libs®
We Wish You a Merry Mad Libs®
Winter Games Mad Libs®
You've Got Mad Libs®

and many, many more!
Mad Libs® are available wherever books are sold